Wetlands

Patti Tana

Papier-Mache Press
Watsonville, CA

Copyright © 1993 by Patti Tana. Printed in the United States of America. All rights reserved including the right to reproduce this book or portions thereof in any form. For more information contact Papier-Mache Press, 135 Aviation Way #14, Watsonville, California 95076.

ISBN: 0-918949-35-1 Softcover
ISBN: 0-918949-36-X Hardcover

Cover art, "Striding Dancer," endless line drawing, © 1982 by Alfred Van Loen
Cover design by Cynthia Heier
Photo by John Renner

Grateful acknowledgment is made to the following magazines for original publication of works included in this collection: *Esprit: A Humanities Magazine, The Fire Island Tide, Hawaii Pacific Review, Hiram Poetry Review, Infinity Magazine, Live Poets, The Long Islander, Nassau Review, The Northport Journal, Ripples: New York Marine Education Association, SCREE, Shooting Star Review, The Sow's Ear, Verve, Wordsmith: A Journal of Poetry and Art*, and *Xanadu: A Literary Journal*.

Thanks and acknowledgment is also made to the following publications which first published or accepted for publication some of the material in this book: *How Odd This Ritual of Harmony* (Gusto Press, 1981) for "The Line," "Stopped at a Light," "Threshold," and "Torn Pictures"; *I Name Myself Daughter and It Is Good* (Sophia Books, 1981) for "Stopped at a Light"; *The Poet's Job: To Go Too Far* (Sophia Books, 1985) for "Torn Pictures"; *American Fiction 88* (Wesley Press, 1988) for "Harbor Island"; *Poetry Center 1989 Anthology* (Passaic County Community College, 1989) for "The Wonders of Infinite Smallness"; *If I Had a Hammer: Women's Work in Poetry, Fiction, and Photographs* (Papier-Mache Press, 1990) for "Found Money"; *The Tie That Binds: A Collection of Writings About Fathers & Daughters/Mothers & Sons* (Papier-Mache Press, 1992) for "Torn Pictures"; *New Covenant* (Birnham Wood Graphics, 1993) for "Calling Up the Moon"; and *Call It Courage: Women Transcending Violence* (Temple University Press) for "Gifts."

Library of Congress Cataloging-in-Publication Data

Renner-Tana, Patti, 1945-
    Wetlands / Patti Tana. -- 1st ed.
        p.   cm.
    ISBN 0-918949-36-X (alk. paper) : $12.00. -- ISBN 0-918949-35-1
(pbk. : alk. paper) : $8.00
    I. Title.
PS3568.E615W48   1993
811'.54--dc20
                                                                    93-24170
                                                                    CIP

Thanks to:

Billy Williams and elaine lynn for their support.

Tony Tommasi for being attuned to my voices.

Sandy Enzer, Elaine Gold, Helen Collins, Bob Karmon, Gene Hamlet, Elise Binder, Renee Goldberg, Toby Lieberman, Bill Fahey, and Anita and Alfred Dorn for their encouragement.

George and Peggy Wallace of Birnham Wood Graphics for their beautiful work in publishing "The River" section as a chapbook.

The Poetry Circle for their helpful responses: Anne Ruth Ediger Baehr, Barbara Lucas, Barry Fruchter, Virginia Terris, Pat Falk, Lois Walker, Mildred Jeffrey, Pat Nesbitt, and circles of Full Moon Women and of friends at work and at home.

Editors Paul Doyle, Maxwell Corydon Wheat, Jr., Hale Chatfield, Don Parker, and Sandra Martz who sent these words to wider circles.

I am grateful to Fay Hovey, Bruce Urquhart, and Nassau Community College (SUNY) for a sabbatical which made possible both the time and the travel that some of these poems and stories required.

To my moorings—
my mother, Ada, who gave me life
John, who shares my life
and especially Jesse, to whom we gave life.

Contents

The Waters of
Childhood

The Book of Clouds

Next to my mother's bed
was a small book of clouds.
She kept it there because
printed on the dark blue cover
in gold letters
was my brother's name.

He was much older than I,
a special guest in white
sailor suit, handsome and smiling
an official smile.
I knew him only well enough
to adore him.

And when he came home we would dance
the Princess Waltz, my feet on top of his,
soles lifted from below,
arms stretched up   up
beyond his long legs to the real smile.

And when he was away I had
the book of clouds,
magic words in boldfaced letters
below hazy forms: **cirrus, stratus,
cumulonimbus.**

Resting on the bedstand
his name—my name—
brought word from a world beyond
the big bed down the hall where
my father made my mother cry.

The Small Bed

In the small bed
in a room made out of tin
I slept.
            When the rain beat sudden
drums on the roof
                    I dreamed.

And when the house was too quiet
when the angry echoes were still
I cried—
    my pillow a raft on the night.

Torn Pictures

I have not seen him since I was ten
but remember his face was big
with stubbled cheeks. Thick hairs
poked from his nostrils.
His scalp was starting to bald
so he'd comb the wisps
back over the space. I don't remember
his eyes or his smile, only his angry
stare and spit through clenched teeth
as he struck me.

I remember too the smell of house paint
he let me scratch off his face
in a moment of gentle holding.
But usually he smelled stale
from cigarettes and whiskey. Years later
when I would kiss a boy through sweaty fumes
of alcohol and tobacco, I would
think of my father.

When I looked through my mother's
yellowed photographs, I found only
torn pictures

> *his young bride, poised, smiling at no one,*
> *me as a baby suspended in my mother's arms—*
> *the other half of the bridge ripped away.*
> *Here and there remains his knee*
> *or his fingers*

ragged edges where he should have been.

Gifts

The first holiday after the divorce, Jack sent us gifts. It was strange and scary because he had never given anything when he lived with us as our father. Never played games or made things with us or sang us a song. We'd lived in a minefield. No matter how careful we were, he'd explode.

We weren't sure whether to accept the gifts, but we didn't know how to send them back.

My little brother, David, played the toy drums with savage insistence. Fred didn't know how to work the hand brakes on the English racer, so he crashed into a parked car on his first ride. The doctor had to wrap his ribs with wide strips of tape.

The gift Jack sent me that holiday is not only lost but forgotten.

About six months later, though, I did have a dream about a crate of oranges from Florida. Fat bright fruit that smelled like blossoms. Attached with wire to the wood slats of the crate was a tag addressed to me from him. Later that day a man stopped my older brother on his way home from school and told him that Jack was living in Florida and was sending us a crate of oranges.

We never received oranges or anything else from him. Never saw or heard from him again—but I still have dreams. Some are the long shadow Jack cast down that narrow hallway and the car that follows me down an endless street.

I used to have dreams born of the terrible longing for a father's love. The night before I delivered the commencement speech, Jack stood in the back of the auditorium, radiant with pride. But when I gave my speech, he was not there.

The night before my wedding I dreamed that Jack came to see me alone in the temple. I stood at the altar and he stood in the doorway. He held no gifts. He gave no blessing. We looked at each other and said nothing. He did not ask forgiveness, nor did I offer it.

Subway

He sees the long legs and the trim
along the edge of her
collar, and thinks a man
could make a go of it
with a woman like that

She feels someone watching
and lays a ribbon across the page
to hold her place
and looks up at the near man
swaying with the motion of the train

He sees her brown eyes and the fine
line of her lip
and he wants that face
to smile at him
and he wants to start again

She looks down to the book in her lap
still seeing the brim of his hat
tipped back
thinking how foolish she is to want
to go dancing
instead of home from work

As the train approaches her station
she rises from the seat
and the stop jolts their bodies together
long enough for them to fumble
apologies giving him the chance
to walk her to her father's
small apartment

By the time the little girl is born
love is long buried beneath his lies
and she is just another
new start that fails

All her wit and all her will
could not move them from the track
they rode

But there is another story
about a daughter
who learned from the mother to love
long after the man is gone.

Silver Dollars

We were poor, but never broke. Hidden beneath a pile of old shoes on the floor of my mother's closet was a black pocketbook full of silver dollars. She had saved them from the tips she earned as a waitress.

When she came home from work, she emptied the coins from the big pockets of her apron onto the kitchen table, and I'd help her sort the pennies, nickels, dimes, and quarters. We'd count them as we stacked them into piles, then stuff them into paper wrappers of red, blue, green, and orange that we'd exchange for dollars at the bank. Usually there were a few half dollars, and these we put aside to spend or, if they were beautiful, save with the dollars. The most beautiful was Liberty striding across the earth in her long loose gown, seven stars above her out-stretched arm, the sun blazing at her feet.

At least once a month Mom would bring home a silver dollar. I would get out the black bag and examine the date and picture of the new addition before I added it to the collection. The eagle stretches out its wings on some, holding them up or down, grasping arrows and a branch in its talons. On my favorite one the wings are folded and the eagle looks away into the distance behind it so I can only see its back. PEACE is written on the mound where it perches. On the other side of the coin is the head of Liberty crowned with rays, her hair flowing back from her face. I'd touch her smooth cheek on one side and the fine rows of eagle feathers on the other, the raised numbers of the date and the letters of the words.

The coins were round and solid and heavy. They were made of real silver and they seemed to be worth much more than the green paper that creased and soiled and tore.

The most I ever counted at one time was a hundred and fifty. When they ran low, down around fifty, I became nervous. Usually the black bag contained about one hundred dollars, and that was enough to give me a sense of security. I knew that when we had to we could dip into the stash and buy a quart of milk, a dozen eggs, and a large loaf of seeded rye bread—all for one silver dollar.

One time when I had my heart set on going to the movies, I was very disappointed that my mother didn't have enough money for me to go. The admission was twenty cents, the same as a quart of milk.

She thought for a minute, smiled, and went upstairs to her room. When she came down she placed a silver dollar in my hand.

"No," I protested, trying to give it back to her. "They're only in case of emergency—for necessities—"

"This is a necessity," she assured me. "The soul needs sweets."

I knew what she meant. She had often told me the story about her father, who we called Papa. It was the Depression. She was raising her first child alone, with whatever help her father could give her. They were shopping together in a crowded grocery store when a young woman placed her selections on the counter, among them a small carrot cake. Quietly she asked the clerk if she could pay the bill at the end of the week.

"No cake for beggars!" he boomed, taking the cake off the counter and putting it back on the shelf. Everyone was stunned into silence.

And then Papa said, "Give her cake. The soul needs sweets."

I took the silver dollar and went to the movies. I even bought myself a chocolate bar with nuts to eat during the show.

Found Money

Almost every day I find
a penny on the street.
And if the penny faces up
I call it luck.
And if it's down
I call it money.

When I was young
I helped my mom clean a store at night
after her regular job.
I'd spray counters with ammonia
that went up my nose and stung my eyes
then rub away the fingerprints
with a soft cloth.
I'd scrape gum from the floors
and hold the pan as she swept
in dust and black dirt.

Sometimes I'd find coins in the dressing room.
I even found a dollar
behind a row of gowns.
No matter if I found a dollar or a dime
Mom made me leave it with a note
on the big wooden register.

Once I found a wallet
on the floor of a movie theater.

No name. No pictures. Only money.
Even in the dark I could see
it was red, smooth plastic red.
I looked at my mother
and she looked away.

Almost every day I find
a penny on the street.
And if the penny faces up
I call it luck,
And if it's down
    I call it money.

Sudden Showers

Sudden showers
promise some relief
this summer afternoon.
Leaning out for spray
the busy sister
takes the time
to watch the rain
shine the dark
green leaves.

Suddenly remembering
the baby brother
in her charge
she runs downstairs
but he's not there.
Out to the yard—
still no brother.
Not frantic yet
she turns to the front
where he is naked
as a chick new hatched
splashing in summer

rain!

Attack Flamingos
for David

My brother called them
Attack Flamingos—
pink plastic birds
on metal poles
guarding the geraniums.

Their menacing glare
protected the plants
behind the tiny white
broken fence
mended with rusty nails
that looked to us
like railroad spikes.

We used to kick that stupid fence
the way we always wanted to
kick small dogs nipping at our feet.
But we never dared
touch the geraniums.

The Flavor of Raspberry

plucked from the tangled
    patch in my yard
clusters of red
    squish sweet in my mouth

seeds in my teeth
    tease my tongue
cuts in my skin
    blood sweet

McKeever's Hill

Behind our house
on Simpson Place where I grew up
an empty lot rose steeply to Smith Street.
From the kitchen I could see the slight
rise of the raspberry patch at the back
of our yard, then the hedge that marked
where our property ended
and McKeever's hill began.

McKeever must have lived
in one of the big houses flanking the hill.
Or maybe he owned the place across the street
from the hilltop before it became
Nardone's Funeral Home.

The spring I learned to walk
Mother watched in the yard as I tested
my legs on the small mound near the berries.
Again and again I'd make my way up
and then run down, laughing even
when I stumbled and fell.

Coming home from school
I'd gallop down the steeper slope or stretch out
sidelong and tumble over and over—
earth,sky,earth,sky,earth,sky
like a rolling pin on a tilted table.
No one ever shouted or shook an angry fist.
No one ever pulled aside a curtain, scowling,
and rapped on the glass.
No one ever stopped me.

In the gathering
shadows of summer evenings, kids played
kick-the-can in front of my house.
We could hide near the houses
but McKeever's was out of bounds.
After play we'd plead for coins
to buy ice cream at the store
up beyond the hill and past
the funeral home.

Much larger than a house,
stark white with black around enormous windows,
Nardone's Funeral Home had wide stone steps
leading up to carefully tended gardens and lawns.
We'd dare each other to peer
through the lace at the men
in dark suits. Still more daring
was a peek into the cellar
that smelled like a hospital.
We'd scrape our feet on the gravel drive
but when black limousines lined the way
we'd sneak by.

Hands full of ice cream
we retraced our path through the funeral
grounds, down the stone steps,
across the street to McKeever's hill shouting
"Race you to the bottom!" and gulped
down the last bit of melting ice cream,
tossing away the stick.

On snowy winter days
children with sleds on the hill were safe
from cars skidding on icy roads.
I'd sit up and steer with my feet
on the wood crosspiece, the rope in my hands.
Or feeling brave I'd lie on my belly gripping
the bar, chips of snow whizzing by,
spraying my face.

When smoky dusk
darkened the white winter sky, I'd slide
down one last time, through the hole
in the hedge and into my own backyard.
Mother would see me from the kitchen
and heat a mug of barley soup
to warm my icy hands.

That winter of my first blood
flowing, I carried my sled up from the cellar
when the first snow fell. As I waxed
metal runners with the white stub
of a candle, Mother said I shouldn't
ride anymore because
I was a woman now.

Climbing McKeever's that day
trailing the sled along, I looked up
at the black-bordered windows.
They seemed to be watching the children
slide down the hill.

The Waters of Childhood

When I think of the waters of childhood, the river comes first to my mind. The streets of Peekskill rose on the east bank of the Hudson River like trees with roots in the water. My house was only two blocks from the river—two steep, long, winding blocks up a street everyone called Snake Hill. In a town built on hills this one was famous. Too treacherous for cars in the ice-covered snow time, Snake Hill was claimed by children sledding all the way down to the railroad station by the river.

The regular click of the wheels on the tracks and the deep-throated cries of train whistles carried my thoughts and sometimes me south along the river to New York City and north toward Poughkeepsie, Albany, and the country beyond.

In autumn we'd ride north to catch the colors at their peak, the red and amber hillsides, their rusty reflections on the water. One fall when I was five, my mother and I rode all the way to Albany to visit my oldest brother, Herbert, at college.

At least once a year Mother took me on the train south to New York City. To catch the southbound train we had to get to the tracks nearest the river: up a long metal staircase, across a narrow walkway high above the tracks, then down another staircase—the wind blowing my skirt. Waiting on the platform, I'd look for the sleek body to come around the wide curve of the river, silent and powerful, then lean as far as I dared toward the tracks to see its approaching face, enormous and loud.

I'd sit by the window and watch the flow of the river as the train swept me along. The water was smooth gray-green if I looked directly sideward out my window, yet shimmering blue if I looked aslant out the window of the seat in front of me. To an eight-year-old that seemed wonderful and strange, but I could not draw my gaze away from the water to ask for explanations. We'd always pass rusting tugboats pushing their huge flat loads. Sometimes I would see on the western shore a silver engine pulling long white cars like the tail of a nearby comet.

In New York City we would go to a museum or a play and then take the train back home from Grand Central Station. After we emerged from the dark tunnel and passed the massive blocks of shadowy buildings, a narrow lane of water reflected whatever light was left in the sky. At first pinched by sheer palisades, the river quickly widened beneath shelves and ridges of gray boulders bulging through masses of trees, and then opened to the smooth layers of the Ramapo Mountains in shades of purple at nightfall.

The train moved swiftly past Dobbs Ferry and Tarrytown, past Sing Sing where my father had served time before he met my mother. I was glad nobody else on the train knew that. Always it paused at Harmon, just above Sing Sing, to change engines. Always the hiss of the steam and the small sudden jolt as the cars coupled. And then the slow, gentle rocking motion of those last few miles home.

When the trees were bare I could see the river from Mother's bedroom window. To the south lay the Ghost Fleet, large gray warships where tons of rotting wheat were stored. Whenever Mother used to say I should finish my meal because people were starving, I wondered why those ships couldn't sail to where their cargo was needed. Northward on the opposite shore was Bear Mountain State Park. On clear winter nights I could see lights outlining the ski jump, and once I saw flames from a skier's moving torch split the dark space between the lights.

Until my parents were divorced when I was ten, we often accompanied Father to his summer weekend job as security guard at Bear Mountain Park, crossing the river westward at the Bear Mountain Bridge. To reach the bridge he drove north over precarious mountain roads, often skirting ledges and stone walls. He made every trip a race—tires screeching, horn blasting—and we were his captives. Mother sat next to him begging him to slow down. In the backseat big brother Fred sat up straight, jaw clenched, knuckles white on the back of the seat in front of him. I crouched down with my arms around little David and peeked out, when I dared, to see how far we had to go. When I saw the river again I knew we were almost safe.

While Father roamed the park grounds in mirrored sunglasses and olive uniform, gun on hip, Mother took the boys and me to the playground, the zoo, the pool, the lake. Hessian Lake, surrounded by tall pines and weeping willows whose slender branches bent way down to the water, was my favorite place.

Sometimes we'd rent a rowboat and take turns rowing across and back, but no one was allowed to swim in the lake. Sometimes the boys would fish from the shore using an earthworm or a soggy wad of bread for bait. When they pulled a small shining body from the water in triumph, I hated to see it thrash in the air, hated to see its mouth torn when they took it off the sharp hook and threw it back.

Near the rowboat landing a plaque explained that the lake was named after the German mercenary soldiers who drowned there during the American Revolution. Hired by the British, they were supposedly invulnerable, but the Colonists sank their boats as they rowed across the lake. Their bodies were never found, giving rise to the legend that Hessian Lake is bottomless. It pleased me to think that here was a place where hired assassins could be made to vanish.

I'd walk around the lake and find a quiet place to sit and look at the reflections in the water. Around the rim the trees doubled in length and color in fluid shadows. The large, moving surface gently distorted the tone of the sky and patches of clouds. Even the slightest breeze gave texture to the water, and sun highlighted the shifting patterns.

If I drew close to look at my own face I would see a pale oval, freckled as a fish. Small earrings where a gypsy had pierced, dark braided hair, teeth in braces that never did close the gap between them. Eyes the same changeable green as the lake, and, like the lake, flecked with gold.

Beneath the surface of the water, another world: fleeting tadpoles and fuzzy moss on oddly shaped stones that looked in shifting, filtered light like tiny forests on small islands. I'd find a stone and see how far I could skim it, or toss it high and wonder how deep it would fall in the water, imagining it falling forever or hovering above a place too deep to reach.

The River

The River

All the bright day I rode my bike along the river
gold flashing among the dizzy leaves
water clear and rushing over stones
the sound drawing me on.

All day I rode with the wind in my face
till I lost a shoe when I drank at the river
and turned to go home.

It was dusk when I entered the old
house on the hill
and you were glad to see me.

You showed me strings you had tied to a stick.
I watched you dip strings in hot tallow
again and again
while the long tapered bodies grew thick.

Then you lit two of your candles
and there in the flickering shadows we stood
between floors on a landing.
You reached to embrace me as I turned toward you

and gently your lips brushed on my lips
and gently your tongue entered my mouth
finding the way through the dark.

I stood open—river swelling inside me—
rising and falling—
walls breathing for me—

the sound of the river rushed in my ears
my legs were water (I might have fallen
if your arms had not held me).

Finally
you turned with a smile as though it were natural
and walked down the stairs
leaving me filled
with that long trembling.

When I could speak I said, *Let's walk by the river.*
Then I asked, *Will you be loving?*
and laughed at my words.
I meant to say, "Will you be leaving?"
and then you laughed too.

A slip of the tongue, you said.
Yes, I said, *a slip of the tongue.*

A Brief Walk

We had time only for a brief walk
long enough to hear the water
moving swiftly over stones—
their bald domes rising from the shallows.

Near the river I found one that fit in my hand,
smooth and dry, split in two.
Inside were dark shapes—
                         two halves of a moist heart.

This Year

let's shake loose the fall
upon our faces
and if it rains
the rain upon our faces.

Let's get lost
with the map in our pocket
and thunder
rumbling our names.

For now I will measure by seasons
my time on the earth: this fall
giving way to winter
till winter sun melts the snow
and swells a mountain spring
where lions come to drink.

Looking at the Fence

We should have stayed
looking at the fence he said
after we drove to the open
bay where apparently random stakes
made patterns in the water.
No gulls perched on the poles
as they did in his memory
but a narrow stick turned
in the wind on top of one.

Spotlights from the pier
seemed to feature the wind
stick and focused our attention
on that spot of light within
a cloudy dusk. Something
in the shape of the dark
hills beyond that he had
not photographed
when he lived there
and that one windy spot of light
undid him.

I miss the birds he said
and something about a child's
toy, then hurriedly drove us away.

No

I will not speak
when words stick in my throat like bricks,
when all words say *love me*
love me as I love you.

I will not speak
when I am feeling like a wall of bricks
that runs along the bottom of a hill
where water seeps.

Touching the wall
moss springs green and soft and moist
and silent as the forest after rain
before birds learned to sing.

No, I will not speak
when I would rather touch.

I Have Touched

your hair
with the palms
of my hands
I have fingered
the strands
around and around

your ears
with my words
I have tickled
with laughter

your neck
with my tongue
with my teeth
with my lips
I have kissed

your thighs
with my thighs
pressing between
ha! I have touched

your feet
your scars
you said you bleed hard
as I traced the soft flesh

your hands
with my hands
your chest

with my chest
and even your heart   yes!
especially your heart

my cheek to your breast
as it rises and falls
my breath in your hair
the wind in the leaves

oh yes these
I have touched.

I Can't Believe the Moon

I can't believe the moon
that hangs above my house
(an empty bowl
slightly tipped)
also hangs above your house.

I understand the turning of the earth
brings sun to you an hour late,
how forecasters say
the whole country will be sunny
—sunlight blazes far away and so immense.

But the moon, the moon appears
shyly from the sea
and shuttles westward through the dark—
a private code to those who know
the patterns of replenishment
and loss.

Last full moon I awoke to the vision
of my room filled with bright shadows
filtered through curtains.
Reaching out my hand I touched the lace
the moon had cast upon your skin.

I keep track of three stars you taught me
form Orion's belt.
When I looked to the end of your pointing finger
(your other arm around my shoulder)
they were just above my yard.

But now they too have traveled west. I fear
I'll lose them soon.

For now it seems everything
turns west. My eyes follow the dropping sun,
and though you're but an hour away
reckoned by the sun,
I can't believe the moon
shines through your bedroom window
as it shines through mine—
        moonlace on your skin.

Old Habits Die Hard: Milk

the way I keep shaking the milk
long after the cream is mixed by machine
long after I started drinking milk
without cream. Pale drops splatter
when the seal is broken.

the way the cat keeps leaping on the screen
clinging white belly and eyes
long after my neighbor said
stop feeding it.

the way I keep reaching for the phone
to lap up your voice
long after you've gone
long after you've gone

Only with Dreams

With only dreams to sustain me
how will I find my way?
I search for you in familiar scenes
but when I ask the day
someone shouts the time scurrying by
and I know I'm late but I don't know
where I have to be
or why.

As I seek through this dream
nourishment
people spring at me
like the traps that click all night
in my kitchen   a death factory.
Usually the throat is crushed
so there is no squealing
and very little blood. But
the eyes   tiny black beads
pop from their heads in utter
astonishment.

A few spill their guts
as they try to tear away
caught in the full throes
of their body.
When just the nose or the tail
or a leg is snapped in the metal
they flail and drag the board around
a futile time
before they die.

What are mice doing in my poem?
They are not in my dream.
I know what bothers me is not their
plaintive sounds waking me from sleep,
nor the grains of cereal
scattered on the shelf, bags of dog food
gnawed open, a few slices of bread
I was saving for breakfast.

I know what bothers me
is the tiny pellets
like startled eyes
they leave in my kitchen—
eyes that find the food,
eyes that fail to see the trap
and feel—too late—
the snap of death. And for what?
A piece of soiled cheese?

Nagged by counter crumbs,
disgusted by the turds in pans,
the cupboard, the oven,
I set the traps
          one after another they'd fall
for it—a piece of cheese on a board
with a delicate wire spring.
I would leave the bloody stains
and clumps of gray fur to warn them
but they kept coming   *three   four*

and then   *seven*
sometimes two a night.

After I killed a baker's dozen
I thought I'd write to you about
the household drama,
knew you'd understand the need,
but they kept coming night after night—
how many
could have run from winter?
eighteen   nineteen   twenty   I checked
the outside of the house for holes
but found none   *twenty-one*   Where
are they coming from? Litters
breeding in the walls?   *twenty-two   twenty-three*

When the toll reached two dozen
I stopped counting
so I can't say anymore
just how many died
or how many more will follow.
What I want to tell you is
the living eat the cheese
from under the nose of the dead.
Not even a dead body can stop
the terrible need
the frantic search.

Perhaps that's why the hungry
mice ate their way into this poem
though they were not in my dream.

And does it matter that in my dream
I find you and you let me suck
and suck your tongue *(More?*
your eyes say *Have*
as much as you need) until I awake
with my eyes overflowing
and my mouth open

White Space

knowing you need to be
in your immediate distance
I explore white space

profile
                    shadow
      aura

imagining the unseen
embracing the intangible
this gift of contradictions

speaking to you
even when I can not
speak with you

Tonight

I conjured up your image
for the first time in months.
You were home, but not one
I recognize—carved in the side
of a mountain, with ivy on rock outcrops
in your backyard where you were fixing me
breakfast. I stopped your busyness to beg
you to be comfortable with me,
not to waste the little time we had.
And you asked, *If you had to choose,*
what would you choose?
And I answered, *To be understood.*
Ah, that you have, you said,
your eyes steady in mine.

Then you were sitting
on the floor in the middle
of a room with a huge dictionary open
before you. We seemed to be
in a hospital ward—narrow metal
beds with thin covers and a woman
in white behind a glass wall.
You were looking up
the word *inclination*
and we were playing
with the meanings. I tried to convey
how it feels to know
the outcome of a fall at the moment
of descent everything shattering
before me and nothing
I can do to stop it.
And you said, *So,*
you understand. And I said, *Yes.*

Western Window

When a new house blocked the trees
I broke through the bedroom wall
and moved my bed west.

Outside the west window
bare gray branches of maple
pointed in all directions.

Through this crazy lattice, two blue spruce
traced the wind with symmetrical limbs,
gold cones dangling in the sun.

And beyond the spruce, the daily show
of clouds and birds and planes
across the shades of sky.

It is spring now, the first
spring through my window. Buds
nipple the branch, then flare.

Yesterday a strong wind sent blossoms
flying and today I can almost touch
the unfolding leaves.

In My Keep

Today's leaves dot the rose of Sharon—
a string of pale green promises
on the cluster of thin gray canes
near the weathered fence. Bubbles
rising skyward from the bottom of a pond.

Soon the sticks will bend beneath the heady
weight of pink and white and purple, nodding
over the picnic table. Then the sepals
that bind blossom to stalk
will dry to cups of parchment.

But today I want to think of how they grow
right up to the house, how they lean into the room
through open windows. And how last summer
I walked in and saw the blooms mirrored
on the potted plant you left in my keeping.

And after that, when winter stripped the garden
and only your hibiscus, the darker kin, stayed green
inside my room, how pleased you were when I called
to say the rose of Sharon's parchment cups
are soft with snow.

Blind Trust

one day we took turns
feeling what the blind could
not see
being led through
doors I never knew existed

the sound of you becoming
the physical world
words the shape
of things and spaces

out on the grassy field
the shower of sun was blood
on my eyelids and the earth
solid   giving   dark   rose
with each step
through me

with you away
distant voices return
laughing familiar
in a fabric of conversations
taking apart the spaces

and in dreams you
turn   nearly maternal
parting the tender folds
your blind eye
finding the red darkness

Street Light

I'd forgotten the streetlight, forgotten
roofs and flat sides of buildings beyond
the curtain formed by the maple.
A strong wind blew all but a few faded leaves
from quaking branches.

Now a light shines through my window,
one sharp point of light
beyond the dark shapes
before the greater darkness.

Other Shores

Wetlands

I
enter
and kneel
in the canoe
a dark fold
in light hands
—balance—
and push
the water back
to move forward
across the bay
shining and buoyant.
Here
no solid land intrudes
between puckered waves
and clouds shaped by wind.
Now and then wings
cross the sky
then suddenly
fall through the surface
of the sea
or a fish flings itself
up and out
and splashes down.
Here I am vast
vast as horizon
where reeds lash
the sky

Makani

You know about the heat
but do you know the wet song of the wind?
    When there is no rain, I listen
        for the wind that makes the sound of rain
            with blade and stalk and leaf.

I've been sleeping on the wind-
ward side for three dry weeks
    yet every morning the clacking of the palms
        wakes me with the patter of rain.

Noon sets my hair aflame
when I walk by the stream.
    Tall grass in the wind's breath
        whispers the rain.

Cane fields line a dusty road.
Green spears bend in the evening breeze
    then wave the wind across the field—
        swelling to a sea of rain.

Hawaiians name their children for the sea:
Nakai—of the sea, *Kainoa*—the sea is free.
    But if I bore a child here
        in the hot Hawaiian night,
            I'd name her *Makani* for the wind

Makani
    for the wind that sings the rain.

Tropical Rain

Folks in Hilo know the rain
    starts with a scent, a sudden cool
        shadow on the mountain

wild clatter on rusty tin roofs
    and then—from the tips of shiny leaves—
        last clear notes.

Pray Maker Creek

races beneath
     irregular
opaque
     islands of ice,
riffling edges
     of sotted leaves
caught in the tangled
     roots and stones
          lining the banks,
cold excited bubbling
     cutting
at the base of the hill.

Watching the current
     swift but silent
beyond windows of winter,
remembering the sweet
     persistent
tumbling rush
     through summer's screen.

Open Window Near the Sea

A gust of wind sails curtains out my bedroom window—
    an open window near the sea.
Through flying lace sun flickers on blue sheets—
        dancing lightwaves
                on the hull of boats.

Fishermen in Fuengirda

At night their lights form
constellations in the harbor.
Before dawn they harvest their catch
in huge patchwork nets.

Their fish, arranged by kind
in shallow bins, point
all directions, lacking dimension,
one eye seeing blindly.

Their sons hustle hash
in Generalissimo Franco Square
where enormous church doors stare
on gold merchants and tourists.

By day fishermen mend nets—
heels held against the strong tug
of the needle, faces crossed by lines,
eyes sharp for tears
in the long sweep of the sea.

Sudden Light

evening shadows the dimming street
when sudden lamps ignite
the underside of gulls

rippling patterns of flight
spark the cobalt sky

Bread

Everyone feeds the fat
white swan, long neck gliding
through the swirling
circus of small birds.
Ducks bob around it—iridescent
decoys in a carnival shoot
tipping heads under
for food. Gulls hover above
shrilling their hunger—
beak open, neck throbbing
and the wild insistent bead
of their eyes on my bread.

The Door Blows Open

The man beside you, roused from sleep,
slams it again, but two small birds
fly in—golden green flutters
sheer as a dragonfly's wing.

You reach to open the window
and another bird lands in your palm
much bigger than the two hovering
by the glass.

Round as a dove, a handful of mist
rising dawn pale from a pond,
the bird bows its head, and its beak
pierces the flesh of your hand.

Head and body bore in and disappear
into your palm—feathers become fur
and the tail the black spike of a rat.

Harbor Island

None of the men spoke after Beth entered the car. No one touched her. No one even looked at her until the driver shut off the engine. Then he took his hands from the steering wheel, slowly turned his body toward the backseat, and stared at her.

Why had she taken the ride?

Her old bike had carried her to the last week of summer, but there wasn't time to fix a flat before work that day so Mrs. Hodge, her landlady, dropped her off at Hester's Diner. The locals Beth waited on there appeared friendly in spite of their New England formality. Though she knew she wasn't one of them, working there as a waitress for the summer had meant she wasn't a tourist. Tonight business was light, so she had a chance to talk with a few of the regular customers. Feeling safe on Harbor Island, she decided to walk the two miles back to her cottage after work. Beth folded her big red apron and stepped into the night.

Nights were often chilly, but this one was warm. Tying the sleeves of her jacket around her waist, she breathed out cooking smells and breathed in the sea. Tips rested securely in the pocket of her cut-off jeans, leaving her free to swing her arms as she walked down the center of the road. She listened to the soft pad of her sneakers and the song of the crickets.

The moon was full enough to light her way in the wide spaces between streetlamps and reflected brightly from her white blouse. It made her bare arms and legs look ivory. She played with the lengthening shadows and pretended a string stretched from the top of her head to the moon so she'd walk tall as the pine trees lining the road. The light frosted their needles, making Beth think she'd like to spend a winter on the island.

Placing a hand on each temple, she combed her long straight hair with her fingers, spread it into a fan—the air cooling her neck—and let it fall on her shoulders.

Yes, it had been a good summer. And now that it was almost over Beth could feel pleased that she had decided to live on her own for the first time. She'd had plenty of time to read poetry and to sit by the shore. The motion of the waves reminded her of wheat fields rippling in the wind, yet the ocean created a vast horizon that she had only dreamed about.

Is that the wind in the trees or the hum of a car? Beth tried to control an old fear. Her father used to follow her in his car after her parents' divorce, so she'd learned to look over her shoulder as she walked. Peeking through the classroom blinds, she'd check to see if his car was parked by the school yard, then sneak out the side door and race the two blocks home—chest aching, lungs burning. Alone in the house, she locked herself in and huddled beneath the kitchen table with her eyes closed.

Better to think about her twelfth summer, the summer her father finally left town. She had discovered a discarded bicycle in her neighbor's yard and painted it white. Her mom bought her a pair of green suede riding pants from the thrift shop. Beth rode that bike all summer as though it were the white stallion she'd always wanted.

Certain now that it was a car she was hearing, Beth moved toward the side of the road to get out of the way. She wished she were on her bike.

Headlights approached slowly, fixing her in their glare.

A man's voice called out, "Need a ride?"

Squinting her eyes, she tried to see past the screen of lights, tried not to feel scared. Before she could answer, a head emerged from the driver's window and she recognized Brian. His family owned the general store, and she had served them at Hester's.

Chiding herself for her fear, Beth took a step toward the car and said, "Brian—hi! My bike is broken so I'm walking back from work."

"Hop in. I'll give you a lift."

Beth had been enjoying the walk—until the car startled her. Maybe she'd been brave enough for one night. And she didn't want to seem unfriendly.

Walking toward the car she said, "Okay. Thanks."

When the back door opened and a young man stepped out to hold the door, Beth moved away in surprise. Looking carefully into the car she saw there were two men in back and two in front. As she hesitated, a voice spoke to her from the passenger side of the front seat.

"Sorry about your bike. Anything I can help you with?"

It was Keith. He also ate at Hester's Diner, and he'd wave to her when they'd pass on their bikes.

"No thanks, Keith. I'll be able to buy another tire tomorrow if the patch won't hold. I just didn't want to chance it breaking again when I had to get to work."

Brian introduced the men in back as his friends. The one holding the door, a lanky fellow like her brother, wore thick glasses that looked too big for his face. She couldn't see the other one clearly. He tipped the visor of this cap and left it low on his forehead.

"I'm staying with Mrs. Hodge on Sweet Hollow Road," Beth said as she slid into the backseat. "Where are you guys going?"

The tall man squeezed in next to her and slammed the door. No one answered her. Brian put the car in gear and began driving slowly down the road. Keith faced forward.

Looking beyond the back of their heads, Beth saw shrubs briefly illuminated by the headlights. Glancing to her left and right she saw that the men flanking her also gazed straight ahead like mannequins. When she moved her feet she heard the dull clink of empty cans. The trousered legs on both sides still touched her though she pressed her thighs together. Wedged between their stiff forms, she focused on the road. *Oh no—how could I have been so stupid?*

They drove in silence past the windmill, past the lightning-scarred tree that was her first landmark when she was learning her way around the island. As they drove past the turn for her street, Beth swallowed a sound that rose in her throat.

Keith looked out his side window for a moment. He switched on the radio, fiddled with the static, and snapped it off. The one with the cap began tapping an irregular beat on the metal window edge. The tall man moved in his seat, and Beth felt the cloth of his slacks withdraw slightly from her skin.

Though the windows were open she didn't have enough air. *Breathe, breathe—breathe slowly.* The hair on her arms lifted in chilly patches and she felt suddenly naked in her shorts and sleeveless blouse.

Tires grated as they turned onto the dark gravel road. She wasn't sure if she was hearing the crash of waves on the beach or her blood pounding in her ears.

When the driver shut off the headlights Beth felt as though she were sitting in a dark theater. Then everything solid fell away. Like a plane's roar, a muffled din expanded painfully inside her head.

When the driver cut the engine Beth thought she knew the strangely familiar sound. The air seemed to be buzzing—like that day in the garden when she had pulled up the weeds—bees! She had tried to outrun them as they swarmed around her. Wildly she raked them from her hair and beat them from her body. As though on cue, they flew back into the hole in the earth. Still she heard a buzz—looking down she had seen a bee fly out of her blouse.

When Brian turned and faced her, his right hand gripped the back of the seat that separated them. Beth met his eyes but she could not read them. Locked in the shadow, she hoped he could see her, really see her. Though her mouth was open, she did not breathe. Terror steeled her.

She continued to hold his stare until Brian lifted his fingers, raised his hand—held it in the air—then broke the silence with a hard slap against the top of the seat. Turning back to the wheel, he started the car with a lurch.

Beth felt dizzy. Her toes and fingers prickled as though they were thawing. Letting out her breath she slumped in her seat, almost relieved that a body was on each side of her.

They didn't touch her. They didn't say anything. None of them even looked at her as they dropped her off at the turn for Sweet Hollow Road.

Beth did not see them in the diner during her last week of work. For a long time she didn't speak about the ride. She never went back to the island. Still, her thoughts often returned to what they might have said to one another when they saw her that night on the road.

Dedication

She stands framed
in the window of the small
room
    To calm herself
she lifts her arms
and sways in the dim light,
hands making shapes
in the silence

Through the bars she sees
another window
where another woman is
shaping the air

Their silhouettes dance
across the dark
courtyard

Afterward she tells me
    —I write for her

Stones

Here I walk on slabs of stone
not paths that lightly spring beneath my feet
and keep my step in rain.

No round stone
to hold in the palm of my hand
and skim across the surface of a pond.

Once I learned there are more
stars than grains of sand
on all the shores of earth.

Here it is not dark enough to see the stars.

Calling Up the Moon

Toss a stone in the water and circles spread across the sky.
Post a sign in the natural food store for women to meet
    on the shore when the moon is full.
One comes dancing over the sand, flinging bare feet before her,
One brings a song, cradling a dulcimer,
One shares a large smooth melon, pale yellow orb
    passing hand to hand, sweet juice dripping, fingers and face
        washing in the sea, licking the salty sweetness on the skin,
One hands out bright scarves that fly after them as they run
    along the water's edge playing tag with the waves,
        a line of women curving like a snake on glassy sand,
One taps a small drum and one rattles a gourd
    and one shakes a tambourine trailing red ribbons
        high above her head.
And all of them bring their laughter
    and everyone brings her dreams.

On this first warm clear night
    the moon rises after dark has fallen.
Before it dims their light, stars appear like promises
    above the women forming mandalas on the shore.
Circles within circles spin with the rhythm of their feet
    and the rhythm of their song.
Sand paintings that move and scatter and remain in the mind.
One then two run into the sea. The others cheer
    then welcome the wet bodies into a circle
        of hands and towels that dry and warm.

Let's call up the moon!
The earth, the fire, the water, the sky
return   return   return   return

Silence. There, spreading on the horizon
    a disk of gold spilling along the surface of the sea.
Higher and higher it becomes a mirror of the circles
    they have been forming all night.
In the shadows of the moon's face, one woman sees the child
    she left sleeping in her mother's care,
One the embryonic curve of her desire,
One her husband's scowl as she walked out the door,
One sees her scars,
One the fragments of her self-destruction,
One the emblem of her ascending wholeness,
One the sea of her own tranquility.
And all of them see the singular beauty that monthly rounds
    into a circle of light.

Natural Bridge
for Louise

In Santa Cruz the ocean carves the coast
into steep cliffs.
Between the jagged half-
circles gouged from the land
sometimes the tide creates
a natural bridge—fragile and rare.

I walk along the cliffs with a woman
whose friendship spans a continent
for nearly twenty years, pacing our steps.
She says the distant blue mountains
are the clearest she's ever seen them.
I comment on the sturdy ground cover
blooming at our feet.

No Guarantees

I'm waiting for the muffler to be fixed—
waiting to see if this lifetime guarantee is a scam
or if they really will make good on the advertisement—
when a guy walks out of the shop and leans over
the big yellow car facing me, leans into the window
and kisses the girl in the driver's seat.
And he keeps kissing her with that open-mouth
head-rocking motion while the kid in the backseat—
maybe two years old—watches them, and then turns
to the toy in his hand, and when he looks back at them
they are still kissing: gray sweatpants pressing
hard against the car door,
blue T-shirt tight on his chest.
Metal is missing from the grill so it looks like
teeth knocked out,
the headlight is held in place
with the same black electrical tape that mends her sunglasses,
and the couple is still kissing—
her blondish curls and his slick dark hair moving
back and forth and around.
In her left hand she balances a white Styrofoam cup
on the door where the window goes down,
and her right hand holds the steering wheel—
cigarette smoldering between her fingers.
His bare arms are behind his back, so only their lips
and tongues and teeth are touching.
Then the kid picks up his bottle and sits there sucking,
watching them kiss.
                    And I figure—whatthehell—
no guarantees, but it looks like love.

Don't

Whatever you do
don't let him in.

Blossoms may open
to the sweet stinging
kiss of the bee

the sea part for Jews
to enter their wandering night

stars burst in showers
that fall through light years

but you—whatever you do—
don't.

The Night I Decided

not to dream about you anymore
I didn't.
But the next night you entered
as a wolf quietly walking
through the walls of my childhood
home, steadily making your way
up the stairs
passing through other places
I have lived.

In my attic you assumed
your human form
holding a guitar and looking
at the distant sea.

I heard the song begin.
No use to bar the door.

Lineaments of Desire

going down from the attic
you hold the ladder
as I descend
the afternoon light

we pause on the porch
to catch the sun as it falls
behind the horizon of houses
and I smile at the flashes
of copper in your beard

in the blinding brightness
you stand between me
and the sun setting
tendrils ablaze

a warm summer breeze
ruffles your hair
and the unbuttoned
loose fitting
striped cotton shirt
that covered your chest
all day in soft folds

as you lift your hand
to lean on the white
stucco wall of the house
the front of your shirt
like the flap of a tent
falls open

a slant ray of sun-
light shadows the hair
on the skin of your arm
and your chest
now bare
draws my glance

my eyes flicker down
to the curve of your breast
and the nipple at the center
of the cheek of your breast

looking away
then glancing again
my eyes alight
where my lips would linger

though I dare not
rest my head on the rise
of your chest
my eyes trace the naked
line of your flesh
to the nipple I would touch
with the tip of my tongue

Marvelous Beast

suspended from
   your animal form
      arms and legs circling
    bodies touching
       then glancing away

the tease of your nearness
   and parting excites me
      and now I am striding
   at ease with your bigness
my pleasure spreading
       in widening spheres

and now we are moving
   faster and faster
      though still unhurried
   knowing this lasts
knowing how far
      we can ride

and now I am
   urging you enter
      the quickening center
   everything in me
       shaped to an O

Lucid Dream: Desert

Hot and dry and stark...I see myself in a busy gathering
on the bleached sand...building small shelters of pole and
cloth...*Is this a bazaar?* the dreamer wonders while the
woman in the dream knows where she is and goes about her task

I see a man setting up his tent near mine...he wears a
long white robe like my own...his face lined with years
of the sun, peering into the night...we help each other
with familiar ease...bind wind-flapping blankets of faded
beige to poles with rope

Are we in a gypsy camp?...we are Bedouins, the dreamer
decides, and then I become the woman...living the dream

Glaring sunlight dims to soft pinks and violets of desert dusk
...the rest of the tribe vanishes...only our two simple
tents stand in the silent expanse

I lie on my back under the canopy on a thin mattress...
relaxed and aware...you walk toward me...stretch out
full length on top of me...your heavy body covers me
completely, chest and thighs...I am completely comfortable
with your weight...as though the sky has come down onto me

Dark night deepens vivid threads of blue and red in faded
cloth...then our tents disappear...I rest between earth
and cloudless starless moonless sky

Your lips moisten my lips...I open my mouth...your
tongue slowly circles between my lips and teeth...circles
the cave of my mouth...ridges on the roof like windswept
sand...soft flesh inside my cheeks

The warmth of your kiss spreads down my body...my throat
becomes a pueblo with terraces and windows and ladders...
my chest a landscape of cliff dwellings...down down through
layers of buried cities...outlines of foundations...ancestral
mounds

Beyond the layers of civilization...beyond the layers of stone
...parting the dense broken layers of stone...you above me
thick as thunder...descending into a sea of fire

Moorings

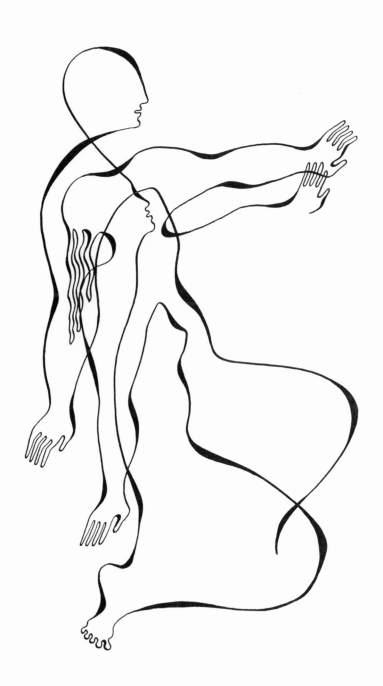

After the Flood

The day we left the mountain
    mist rose from drenched hay
        water beads sparkled in cornfields.

Floods broke bridges
    so we had to poke till we found
        dry ground to cross.

All day the sun smoldered in the gray sky.

At evening it turned a great luminous peach
    then a shadowy strand of damp hair
        I brushed from your forehead.

You Bring Me Back

You bring me back
with a smell
a shape
to my early pleasure.
Deep in the night
I climb the high
chair of your lap
and rest in sure
familiar dreams.

When I turn, you turn
and I become host
to your sleeping
body, your naked body.
Kneading the flesh
aligning the bones
till morning arouses
a shape, a smell
and we turn to each other
in familiar pleasure.

The Line

When I conceived
you, a line
marked my belly
down from my navel.

Darker with the growing
months—a lifeline trailing
from the spot that showed
I had been born
to the place of your birth.

I contemplated the trail
the way
others consider the head
of a pin
counting angels
seeking enlightenment.

When the line faded
after your birth
then disappeared, I was
disappointed.

Now three straight hairs
just below my navel
and shiny patches
from the stretching of my skin
sign your first home.

Nest

Winter and summer
our son joins us as day breaks
—a nest of baskets.

Stopped at a Light

Stopped at a light, I see my son's baby-sitter
step from her school bus and cross the street.
I am about to offer a ride when
the wind catches her hair
and the bright flurry catches my throat.

Her hair is the light brown color of my child's
—the low December sun fires it yellow and red
burning my eyes.

Then I notice a boy walks beside her
not holding her hand but pointing at something
and looking in the same direction.

I cry. Unaccountably, I cry. Not the sobbing
heaves of sorrow, nor the dull moan of depression,
but a welling of memory denied
and wonderful confusion.

I pull into the station and pump my gas. This girl
halfway between my child's age and mine, poised
in that leap—

What else? I turn back and notice something
besides the hair—the jacket open (perhaps
winter will never come this year), the shoulders
back, the breasts comfortable on the chest (I,
still slouched from my childhood tallness, my early
prominences, my ill-fitting bras, notice).

And the scarf—not bandaged round her neck like mine—
tossed   flowing   her feet never touch the street.
The health, the ease, the modest confidence.
I smile.

Driving home I remember my life is only half lived.

Night Songs

your sudden touch
        on my sleeping skin
     more startling than birds
          singing at night

the humming
        bird draws deep
    within the red blossom

when the fluttering leaves
      a fleck of down
    drifts in the current
         above my bed

Sunday Morning

I wake to the smell
of mandarin oranges
and seeds in my bed.

Seeds

We finally got around to planting sunflowers.
Along the back fence most formed puny stalks,
ankle high, with shells stuck on top like paper hats.
Three grew knee high
then fell on their faces in comical flops.

Along the side fence one giant golden head
nodded over weathered wood all of August.
We meant to take a picture, but never did.
This fall John built a darkroom in the basement.
Next year we'll be sure to take pictures.

We had enough tomatoes to feed the neighborhood—
gazpacho and sauce and salads all summer, then
the last green ones rescued before the frost.
I soaked basil and cucumbers in vinegar,
froze parsley and dill for winter soup.

Blue morning glories flourished, but I had to catch them
before they puckered against the sun.
Virginia gave me seeds from her night-
blooming moonflowers
so something was always opening.

I saved the seeds,
labeled blue envelopes,
and stored them in a shoe box in the darkroom.

Two Trees

One stands up straight, yet not so straight it lacks
fullness. The yard so small this one fills a corner.
A maple, its leaves turn brown without flaming
but all summer long it gives me green.

The other leans way over toward the house, a canopy
that filters sun and fans the wind across the yard.
I don't know the name of the one that leans, but it yields
small white flowers in spring, black berries for summer birds
and tongue-shaped leaves that yellow and fall.

Both are rooted in the southwest corner, not far apart.
The maple must have taken first to make the other stretch
so wide for light.
Without these two the yard would be empty.
Together they are my woods.

Thanksgiving

one brown triangle
bound to the branch
after the rest

are fallen

this leaf
this kite
this flag

flying

Before 8 A.M.

No saws   no hammers
lawn mowers   hedge trimmers   edgers   blowers
no cutting down or building up.

Only the ocean's roar
and the soft whoosh of wind fanning leaves.
Only the caw of a fat black bird
too big for the swaying branch.

It's the law.

Walk in the Morning

Steam rose
   from the rain-soaked wood
      where sun struck full on the fence.

I press my cheek
   to the warm moist grain
      and walk with a kiss on my face.

Penny

As she tripped over the corner of her front doorstep, Penny grabbed at the hedge to break her fall. She saw a tumbling kaleidoscope of road, trees, houses, sky. When they stopped she lay still on her back, trying to sense if any bones were broken.

I'm okay, she thought, *only a scraped leg, a sore arm. Good. I could have been laid up for months like Karen.* The year before, her friend had slipped on the ice in front of the health food store and fractured her ankle. While she was healing she went into debt, her fiancé deserted her, and she got fat.

Looking at the broken twig clutched in her hand, Penny laughed to herself and threw it into the bushes—*Grasping at straws.* She had wet herself when she lost her balance, and now she felt the warm wetness on her thighs. The sensation brought back the times after school when she had fumbled with the house key in the locked door and couldn't make it to the bathroom. Her brothers used to tease her about being a "bad Penny," but her mother told her she was a "lucky Penny" who would always land with her head up.

Now her head was propped against the hedge, her cotton skirt bunched up around her hips, and her long bare legs sprawled out in front of her like a wounded flamingo's. A few houses down the street a man who was putting out his garbage seemed unconscious of her flying fall. Cars passed near her house without slowing. The letter carrier was just coming around the far end of the street.

Penny stood up carefully, examined the raw scrape on her left shin, then walked slowly into the house to wash off blood and dirt and to change her underwear.

The bathroom mirror reflected a sharp scratch extending from her left eyebrow down the side of her face in a thin red line. *How dramatic! Certainly will add character.*

Looking closer she saw tiny creases puckering around the new cut, joining the crow's-feet at the corner of her eye. Lately friends had been commenting that the silver in her hair made the brown look frosted. She fluffed up her hair with her fingers and regarded her image in the mirror.

"Could have poked out that eye," Penny said out loud with a wink that was half shudder. Her eyes were hazel green with sparks of yellow and orange radiating from the pupil. She switched on the light above the mirror and watched the quick closing of the dark center.

Whenever she had a close call she thought of the day she'd turned the corner onto Division Street. Feeling like a big girl at ten, she was walking to town alone to meet her mother after work. Penny knew her mom would buy her a treat as they walked home together, usually a chocolate ice cream cone, but the adventure of town meant even more than the treat.

As she rounded the corner by the County Trust Bank with its marble pillars, a car packed with teenage boys stopped next to her. The passenger in the front seat, his mouth twisted in a mean smile, poked a rifle out of the open window and aimed it at her face.

Penny stared into the hollow eye of the gun the way a deer becomes transfixed by the lights of an oncoming car. Stunned—she hadn't cried out or run.

A long moment passed before she heard the snap of the trigger. No shot had fired. Then all the boys laughed and drove on.

Penny remembered how her heart had started beating again, the cold shiver echoing out of her. When feeling came back into her legs and the unseeing passersby became real again, she continued walking the long block to her mother's store. In the years that followed, she often reflected on what happened that day, thinking, *The rest is a gift.*

Relieved that her flying fall caused no serious injury, Penny's thoughts moved to a trip she and her husband had taken to Yosemite when their son was an infant. The baby had woken up early so they decided to catch the sunrise over Half Dome. On top of the mountain, hang gliders were hitching up their harnesses and spreading out wing-shaped sails. Just as the sun became visible over the sheer cliff of the mountain, they leaped. As their bright cloth billowed, a rush of air filled her body, and she'd felt herself soaring above the valley on silk wings. Closing her eyes now, Penny felt again the exhilaration of that flight.

She opened the mirrored door of the medicine cabinet, took out the peroxide, and watched it bubble on her flesh. She squeezed aloe cream onto her palm, rubbed her hands together, and smoothed them over her face, neck, arms, and legs.

I must have rounded that corner hundreds of times—thousands of times. What was I so preoccupied with? Oh yes. She had been on her way to save the azaleas in the front garden enclosed by the hedge. The previous evening she had noticed that wild vines were strangling them, keeping some branches from blooming. By then it was too dark to pull out the vines by their roots, but it had stayed in the back of her mind to take care of the next day.

Aware of every step, Penny walked out the back door and down the driveway toward the azaleas, steering clear of the place where she had stumbled, the skin on her leg tight and her left shoulder sore. When she reached the mailbox, she looked through the letters for any surprises.

The Wonders of Infinite Smallness

Halfway around the world you
send news of our son's thoughts
on infinite smallness—
how all things can be
made smaller, how the tiniest
particle can be reduced to the point
where we cannot see it, how
the universe could have exploded from a speck
and perhaps now the whole
world containing all that
exists could be compressed to the size
of a golf ball,
and would it all be miniature
or scrunched like scrap cars.

Halfway around the world I
miss you both, miss being home.
On a journey for a month to a distant country
retreat, I feel close when I read your words.
And the photograph you sent of our son
holding his newborn cousin,
cradling the small body in his now big hands,
I placed against the mirror of the night-
stand at the foot of my bed.
His eyes
look back at me,
head tilting slightly, strands of hair
falling on his forehead,
lips curved in a wonderful smile.

My host had placed a wooden Buddha (serene
hands cupped in lap) next to the mirror,
and now this picture balances the statue.
Reduced from the original, composed of charm
particles of black and white and silver grays,
his picture grounds me. When I call home
he says, "Are you safe?" and wonders
how our voices fly across the sea.
I tell him about the calf mooing for its mother
in the neighboring meadow
while she is down the road bellowing back.
And as we speak I feel you both
could be in this room, so small
the distance.

For My Son Who Wants to Be Rich

Rich is

toilet paper in the linen closet
when you need it

milk money in the blue cup by the phone

a closet   a phone   a blue cup.

Bequest

after the confusion of being
gripped by the throat on the school bus
Jew words spit in his face
say you're a Jew—say it—
    say Hitler was right!

after the shame of looking away
when teammates mocked kids in beanies
at play across the field
and learning to laugh at jokes
he didn't get
    and didn't want to

he found himself fleeing his nightmare
where boots kicked down doors
women cried aloud
and the graybeard pointed at his back
    running from the house of horror

cursing me for cursing him
    with the burden of his story

after this dream he came to be
friendly with a neighbor
and walked with him three times to shul
and home to bless the bread
    and talk around the *shabbos* candles

now tonight he invites me to temple
where we sit in the solitude of light
deepening gold to red as one by one
just enough gather to sing aloud

and he is proud of being
        the necessary one

perhaps another day may find a boy
running to his door at evening
calling him to stand with nine
who want to say a kaddish
        though he may not return till then

he says he's gonna make a million
        and I wish him luck
tonight it is good to know
        my son made a minyan

In the Doorway

Standing in the doorway, afraid
of breaking his sleep,
I listen to my son's labored breath.

The first time I cradled him in my arms
I watched the sun rise along the spine
of the tall pine across the way.

And the first time he was sick
I ran the shower for steam
and held his head up all night.

Now he thinks he's too old
to be told when
to go to bed, when to wear a hat.

Back in my bed I try not to think
of the lifeless child my friend found
in the crib.
        He saw his son
stand alone just once—
one triumph over gravity.

Toward morning
I listen at my son's door again
and he is snoring like an old man.

Pendulum

*a body suspended from a firm support
so that it swings easily back and forth
influenced by gravity and the spring*

The hour in my son's room is always
three. A modern clock of brass and glass
hangs on his wall. Below the face
a pendulum swings in time—
but the hands don't move.

We changed the battery, fiddled with gears.
I offered to return it for one that works.
No, he said, he doesn't need it to tell the time.
The swinging pulse keeps him company
like at Bubba's house

where the grandmother clock clicks away,
chiming on the hour and the half.
There he learned to count the hours,
the filigree hands pointing
toward the graceful numbers.

When she is gone, the time-
keeper will be his to keep.
Last week she taught him
to set the hands, to hold the weights,
to keep the big clock wound.

Yard Sale

My mother, at eighty, is in excellent health. She survived the years of strife that gave her ulcers, the threatening pap smear, and cancerous patches on her face. Her feet are calloused and distorted with bunions from working long hours as a waitress, salesclerk, and corrections officer to support four children—with the periodic interference of her first three husbands. (My mother the optimist!) She struggled to keep our home together and send my brothers and me to college. Then she went to college, became a teacher, and now she tutors. At eighty my mother has survived the death of two of her children, and every day she still puts a flower in her silvery white hair.

So she surprised me when she said she was planning to have a yard sale and asked me to pick out the things I would keep if she died: candlesticks, vases, bowls, copper kettles, cups and saucers, ceramic birds and animals. And everywhere figurine couples bowing and dancing and sitting and working together, a girl with a basket and a boy with a hoe—images of coupled harmony that she yearned for and that eluded her except for a brief late love and fourth marriage a few years ago to her "sweet Al." She survived even the sadness of his death. Through the years she surrounded herself with these objects from gift shops and yard sales, saying, "They're beautiful, they keep me company, and they don't ask for food or rent."

But they did need dusting. When I was a child I'd try to wipe around them on the knickknack shelves. For a thorough job, I'd hold them up and see light sparkle through the glass, admire the patterns and designs in the delicate china—a woman's face, grains of rice.

And they needed to be wrapped carefully and carted down to Florida when her third husband wanted to retire there, and after he died they were packed again and shipped back up north when she bought a house four blocks from where I live now.

That was fourteen years ago. When she returned north I had just given birth and was desperate for help so I could go back to teaching knowing that my son was in loving hands. Caring for him has given my mother the chance to do the things she'd missed doing for her children when we were young, while he's had the benefit of growing up in two homes, his parents in one and his Bubba in the other. I've had the pleasure of being the link between generations and getting to know my mother as a friend. And I can still walk into my mother's house, search through the refrigerator for something to eat, and reach for a plate that I recognize from "home."

That's why I felt uncomfortable at first about the sale: "You're not dying yet. You have years to enjoy living with your things."

"I don't want scavengers rummaging through them when I die. I'd rather give them away or sell them now and spend the money with you than have them sold for a quarter or thrown away later. Leave the books in case I can't get to the library and leave the plants. The rest can go."

Last year she arranged her funeral and paid for it, and now she was helping me sort out her things. But I insisted that she keep what she loved as well as what I wanted to have in the future. We traced the lineage of each piece as we culled the shelves. Some we put aside to give to people we knew would like them. I chose only what I'd use or display or couldn't part with: "Those dishes Miss Shutter brought from England....I remember playing with that tea set."

The ones that remained in their uncluttered space looked majestic.

The ones we put out for sale on the tables looked different too. Better. Suddenly I saw them as though I were browsing in someone else's yard. If she were not in the process of scaling down, I would have bought most of them for my mother. Throughout the day I'd spot things with new eyes—a carnival glass bowl, a clay bird in a clay nest—and bring them back into her house. A few times I saw a prospective buyer looking at something and I snatched it away before she could buy it. When a customer accidentally broke the head off a youthful lute player, I rescued his mate. Her kick had always seemed mincing. Now dancing alone to her own music, castanets in hand, skirt swirling, she became a gypsy and I chose her for my own.

And how to set a price? My mother turned down an offer for a dozen items from a woman she suspected was an antique dealer, then sold them individually for less to folks she thought would appreciate living with them. She told the buyer the history of each item she sold: "I carried that green bowl on my lap all the way from Arizona....Those glasses are over fifty years old." One of her neighbors collects owls, the little girl across the street collects clowns, and these she gave to them as gifts.

We were busiest at noon when I turned and saw Stan, my neighbor, buying a plate from my mother. It was one I'd considered keeping: pale green and pink with clusters of white apple blossoms. When I went over to him he handed me the plate saying, "I didn't know this was your mother's house. Here. I bought this for you because I thought you'd like the spider's web." Holding the plate up to the sky, I saw again the lightly painted gray web connecting the blossoms.

All day the sky threatened, but the weather stayed dry and comfortably cool for the end of August. During a lull my mother turned to me and said, "These years living near you have been my happiest."

At the end of the day we stored the unsold things in her garage. She said she felt satisfied with what she'd let go of and with what she'd earned. "Now let's go out to dinner with the profits!"

We went to our favorite Chinese restaurant, a quiet place where we had shared each other's luncheon specials many times through the years. But when our regular waiter handed us the menu, my mother waved it away saying, "No menu tonight, Joe." Then turning to me, she said I should order anything I wanted.

"Ah, a little celebration for mother and daughter," Joe said, looking from my mother to me.

I ordered lobster Cantonese and she ordered sesame steak with vegetables. While we were waiting for our meal we clicked our tea cups together and my mother made a toast: "To next spring, when we'll have another yard sale."

Taking her hand across the table I said, "Mom, why don't you do something special with the rest of the money from today's sale."

"I am," she smiled. "I'm putting it away for your old age."

When I came back to my house, I looked at the windows where I'd arranged plants, glass trays, and bottles—cobalt blue, cranberry, amber— and I made a place in the kitchen window for the plate my neighbor bought for me. As I wash my dishes I can see the web.

Palm Reading

Gypsies traced a troubled childhood
and early independence
in the creases of my palm. My life
would be eventful and long—
one said difficult but worthwhile.

I was to have two children
(one died inside me,
the other stands beside me)
and three great loves.

They always saw the same three
great loves. At first I thought
three was many, but now
I wonder: is three enough
for a life so eventful and long?

And maybe love means something other
than a man's voice calling
up my dreams.
                Maybe it means passion
        that opens the sky
            and shows me how
                    stars are formed

The Naked Eye

can see the morning
star through bare limbs
of the sycamore
looking
for all the world
like Christmas in November

can see the flaking trunk
blotched gray
pale green and tan
seeming peeled
more fragile
since leaves have fallen

can see the earth stretch out
from where I stand
rooted
like the morning star
amid the moving sycamore

Passing Around the Skull

Passing around the skull I thought
how wasteful to have my body
burned. Better to give
what's useful to bodies in need,
the rest to an anatomist.

And when my skin is all peeled off,
muscles stripped,
hang my skeleton in a science class
where students learn
to read my bones
and wiggle teeth still rooted in my jaw.

I should like a girl to poke
her finger in the sockets
where my eyes were, wondering
what I had seen and what she
will see before her flesh is gone.

Touched by Zero

No matter how many
march along the rim of the hill
zero follows like a hungry shadow

Patient steadfast absolute
it collects the bill
charged at birth

One brother then two
One two three fathers
A child in my small round womb

Any one touched by zero
equals zero
in time

Summer Storms

This storm reminds me of another. Years ago
I took shelter at my brother's
after I'd lost the child.
                        Thunder woke us
all except my niece who'd dragged her sleeping
bag out to the porch and made a den
where she could see the stars. Instead
jagged streaks lit voluminous clouds.
My brother scooped her up and held her
against his chest while she slept
through the booming storm, her face
nuzzled in his neck. Her damp hair
matted on his cheek was dark
as the rabbit she'd let me stroke that day.
Proud of its beauty and clearly in love
she freed the gentle feral creature
from its cage. Then from the safety
of her embrace offered it for my touch.

Now this storm long beyond that time
when tenderness was balanced in their arms
brings me back to feral creatures
and my brother's sudden show
of love electrified in flashes.

Weight

After walking with Helen through green
meadows, earth yielding to our step,
we part as she turns toward her home
and I toward mine.

Inside the old house I see trees
through every window's wavy glass
and think how lovely
to stay here forever watching the seasons
flower and flame.

Moving through comfortable rooms
I meet a man composed
of men I've known, and he asks,
"Do you feel the weight of the world
will be less when you leave?"

as though he knows my body
has been drifting away—
I've been squinting at numbers and wincing
when I touch the surgeon's cut.

Again I find myself walking toward home
carrying my nearly-grown son
in my arms, but he is a miniature
of himself
        and he is light
lighter than when he was born.

He grows to full size
when I place him in the center
of the bed. I tuck the quilt around him
and watch his breath
rise and fall.

Threshold

Well I remember
       her holding me, rocking
me awash in soft silent
          darkness and sound

Before I was born
       I breathed in her water
salt on my skin
          my body becoming

A child I felt
       breathed in me too
well I remember
          crying out *Mama*

At the last threshold
       well I hope to remember
that same reservoir
          home of all waters

Patti Tana

Patti Tana grew up on the Hudson River in Peekskill, New York. After attending Hiram College and the University of Missouri, she settled in Long Beach, Long Island, to work and raise her family. She is Professor of English at Nassau Community College (SUNY) where she has taught since 1971.

Ms. Tana was elected to the Poetry Society of America and served on the editorial board of *Esprit: A Humanities Magazine*. Currently she is on the editorial board of the *Hiram Poetry Review* and the *Long Island Quarterly*.

As a member of the Womenfolk Song Project, Ms. Tana helped produce and sang on an album of women's work songs, *The Work of the Women* (1975).

The author's previous books are: *How Odd This Ritual of Harmony* (Gusto Press, 1981); *Ask the Dreamer Where Night Begins* (Kendall/Hunt Publishing Company, 1986); and *The River* (Birnham Wood Graphics, 1990).

Patti Tana's poems have also appeared in *When I Am an Old Woman I Shall Wear Purple*; *If I Had a Hammer: Women's Work in Poetry, Fiction, and Photographs*; and *The Tie That Binds: A Collection of Writings About Fathers & Daughters / Mothers & Sons* (Papier-Mache Press).

Alfred Van Loen

Alfred Van Loen was born in Germany in 1924 to Karl and Hedwig (née Jaeger) Lowenthal and died this year. At a young age Alfred was sent to school in Holland, and his parents joined him there when they fled the Nazi persecution of Jews. After graduating from the Royal Academy of Art in Amsterdam, he emigrated to the United States.

The artist's drawings and sculptures are part of the collections of the Whitney Museum, the Museum of Modern Art, the Metropolitan Museum of Art, several Dutch museums, the National Museum of Jerusalem, and the Louvre. He taught at Vassar, Columbia University, Hunter College, the Brooklyn Museum Art School, and for the last thirty years at the C.W. Post campus of Long Island University.

Mr. Van Loen made his home in Huntington, Long Island, where he and his wife, Helen, raised two children.

Quality Books from Papier-Mache Press

At Papier-Mache Press our goal is to produce attractive, accessible books that deal with contemporary personal, social, and political issues. Our titles have found an enthusiastic audience in general interest, women's, new age, and Christian bookstores, as well as in gift stores, mail order catalogs, and libraries. Many have also been used by teachers for women's studies, creative writing, and gerontology classes, and by therapists and family counselors to help clients explore personal issues such as aging and relationships.

If you are interested in finding out more about our other titles, ask your local bookstores which Papier-Mache items they carry. Or, if you would like to receive a complete catalog of books, posters, T-shirts, and sweatshirts from Papier-Mache Press, please send a self-addressed stamped envelope to:

Papier-Mache Press
135 Aviation Way, #14
Watsonville, CA 95076